14 OCT 2011

THE WORLD'S FASTEST MACHINES

Marcie Aboff

www.raintreepublishers.co.uk
Visit our website to find out
more information about
Raintree books.

To order:
☎ Phone 0845 6044371
🖷 Fax +44 (0) 1865 312263
🖳 Email myorders@raintreepublishers.co.uk

Customers from outside the UK please telephone +44 1865 312262

Edited by Nancy Dickmann and Megan Cotugno
Designed by Jo Hinton-Malivoire
Picture research by Tracy Cummins
Originated by Capstone Global Library
Printed and bound in China by CTPS

ISBN 978 1 406216 87 5 (hardback)
15 14 13 12 11
10 9 8 7 6 5 4 3 2 1

British Library Cataloguing in Publication Data
Aboff, Marcie.
The world's fastest machines. -- (Extreme machines)
629'.046-dc22
A full catalogue record for this book is available from
the British Library.

Acknowledgments
We would like to thank the following for permission
to reproduce photographs: ©2009 Kawasaki Motors
Corp., U.S.A pp. **24**, **25**; AP Images p. **23** (Anthony
Devlin/PA Wire); Corbis pp. **6** (© David Madison),
9 (© George Tiedemann/GT Images), **17** (© G.
Bowater), **18** (© Xiaoyang Liu), **22** (REUTERS/Daniel
Munoz); Getty Images pp. **4** (Jon Feingersh), **8**, **16**
(Gilles Mingasson), **19** (China Photos), **21** (MANAN
VATSYAYANA/AFP), **26** (STAN HONDA/AFP), **27** (Joe
McNally); NASA pp. **5**, **13**, **14**, **15**; Shelby SuperCars
pp. **10**, **11**; Shutterstock p. **7** (© digitalsport); US Air
Force p. **12** (Judson Brohmer); Zuma Press p. **20** (©
596/Most Wanted).

Cover photograph of F-22 Raptors reproduced with
permission of US Air Force (Master Sgt. Kevin J.
Gruenwald).

Every effort has been made to contact copyright
holders of any material reproduced in this book. Any
omissions will be rectified in subsequent printings if
notice is given to the publisher.

Disclaimer
All the Internet addresses (URLs) given in this book
were valid at the time of going to press. However, due
to the dynamic nature of the Internet, some addresses
may have changed, or sites may have changed or
ceased to exist since publication. While the author and
Publishers regret any inconvenience this may cause
readers, no responsibility for any such changes can be
accepted by either the author or the Publishers.

Some words are shown in bold, **like this.** You can find
out what they mean by looking in the glossary.

Contents

The world's fastest machines

Ready, set… before you can say go, these machines are speeding off! The extreme machines in this book are fast and powerful. They race around tracks, zip through the sea, and blast across the sky!

Learn more about the space shuttle on page 15!

Formula 1 racing cars

Formula 1 racing cars are fast! They have one seat, no roof, and a powerful engine at the back. They have "wings" at the front and back to give them extra speed. Grand Prix Formula 1 races are held all over the world.

wing

Top speed
413 kph
(257 mph)

NASCAR racing cars

NASCAR racing cars zoom around the race track. They are shaped like normal cars. But powerful engines make them really fast! Roof flaps stop them from rolling over at high speeds.

roof flaps

Top speed
392 kph
(244 mph)

EXTREME FACT
The temperature of a NASCAR car can reach 60° Celsius. Some drivers sweat so much they lose up to 4 kilograms during a race!

SSC Ultimate Aero

For a super fast street car, the SSC **Ultimate** Aero is hard to beat. With a 1,183 **horsepower** engine, it reaches 96 kph (60 mph) in only 2.8 seconds. Most other street car engines have about 200 horsepower.

Top speed
413 kph
(257 mph)

You can buy this fast car for just £400,000!

SR 71 Blackbird

The SR 71 Blackbird is a special type of aeroplane. It flies faster and higher than any other **manned** aeroplane. The pilots even have to wear the same suits that are used for space flights!

Top speed
3,500 kph
(2,200 mph)

EXTREME FACT

The NASA X-43A plane goes even faster than the Blackbird. It also flies without a pilot!

Space shuttle

A space shuttle blasts off with the help of two huge rockets. The rockets later drop off and the space shuttle carries on without them.

Top speed
28,000 kph
(17,500 mph)

The shuttle lands with the help of a **parachute**.

EXTREME FACT

Pushing off from Earth so fast creates pressure from **gravity** known as **G-forces.** Astronauts have to wear special "g-suits" so they don't become ill.

TGV train

France's TGV train takes 2 hours and 20 minutes to travel more than 480 kilometres. That's almost twice as fast as an average train! The ride is so smooth, most passengers don't realize how fast they are going.

EXTREME FACT

TGV stands for "Train à Grande Vitesse." That's French for "Very Fast Train."

Top speed
322 kph
(200 mph)

Maglev train

The Maglev train's speed is powered by magnets. Instead of tracks, the train "floats" on a **magnetic** path. Most Maglev trains have no wheels and no engine noise. The ride is smooth and quiet.

Top speed
581 kph
(361 mph)

magnetic path

Suzuki Hayabusa motorcycle

The Hayabusa is one of the fastest sports motorbikes on the road. It can **accelerate** from 0 to 305 kph (190 mph) in less than 20 seconds. The bike speeds forward and the front tyre jumps off the ground. Drivers need to be very careful to avoid getting hurt.

Top speed
317 kph
(197 mph)

Earthrace boat

The Earthrace boat broke the world record for circling the globe. What makes it go so fast? Fat! Earthrace uses **biofuel** and animal fat. The fat makes the Earthrace boat fast. It is better for the environment, too.

Top speed
74 kph (46 mph)

Kawasaki jet ski

Riding the Kawasaki Ultra 260 feels like "flying" on water. It can go much faster than other jet skis. The Kawasaki's engine produces the power of engines twice its size.

Top speed
112 kph
(70 mph)

Kingda Ka roller coaster

The Kingda Ka is one of the world's fastest roller coasters. This "scream machine" goes from 0 to 206 kph (128 mph) in 3.5 seconds! The Kingda Ka **accelerates** twice as fast as some racing cars.

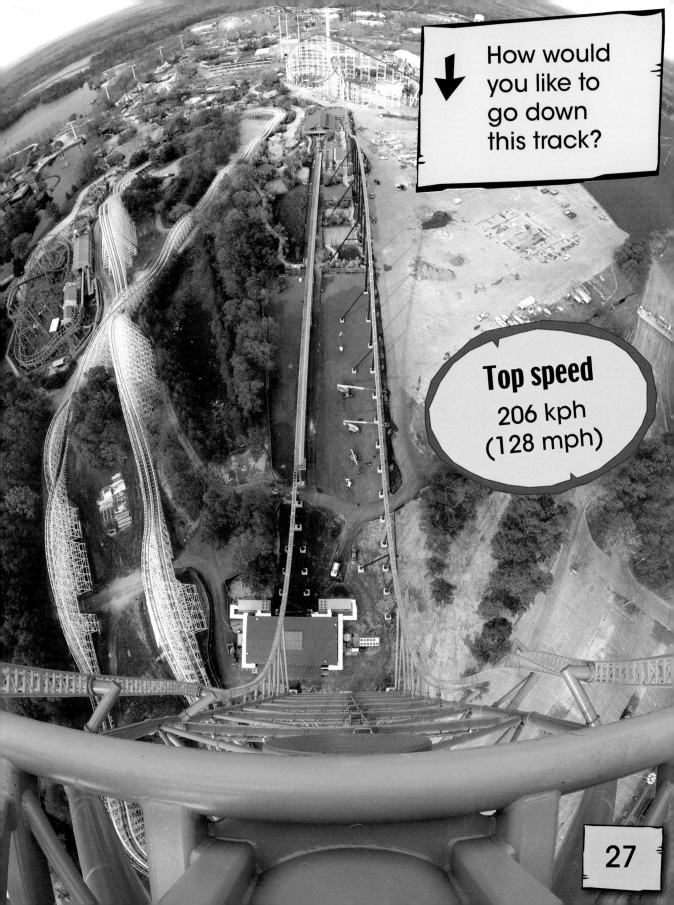

How would you like to go down this track?

Top speed
206 kph
(128 mph)

Test yourself!

Try to match each question to the correct answer.

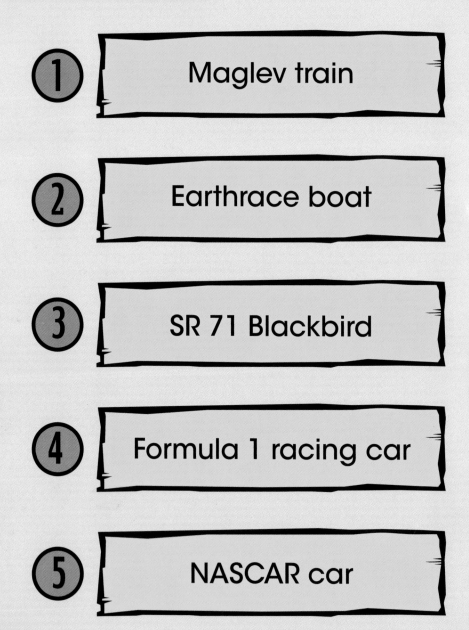

① Maglev train

② Earthrace boat

③ SR 71 Blackbird

④ Formula 1 racing car

⑤ NASCAR car

a Which machine is powered by fat?

b What is the fastest **manned** aeroplane?

c Which cars have "wings"?

d Which machine is powered by magnets?

e What super fast cars have roof flaps?

Glossary

accelerate to move faster or speed up

biofuel a fuel that comes from vegetable sources

G-forces the force of gravity or acceleration on the body

gravity the force that holds things down on Earth

horsepower a unit of power

magnetic something that can be pulled towards a magnet

manned aeroplane that is flown by a person

parachute sail-like object that catches air; used to slow something down

ultimate greatest

Find out more

Books

Formula 1, Stephen Rickard (Ransom Publishing, 2010)

Spacecraft: World's Fastest Machines, Charles Hofer (Powerkids Press, 2008)

Speed Machines, Paul Harrison (Powerkids Press, 2008)

Websites

Formula 1
http://www.formula1.com/
The official Formula 1 website.

Space shuttles
http://www.nasa.gov/mission_pages/shuttle/main/index.html
The space shuttle information page on the NASA website.

Earthrace boats
http://www.earthrace.net/
The official website of the Earthrace boat.

Find out

When did the Space Shuttle *Endeavour* launch?

Index